# THE COLORADO MINE COMPANY

THE SHIP'S WHEEL

SULIVAN'S old place

todd's

**MARKET STREET EXCHANGE**

Fran' Brien's

n

Perry's

Maisone

Carlos'n Charlie

**TRADER VIC'**

BlueBoar Inn

dobsol

Crisis opkins

THE Pimli

**BENSON & HEDGES 100's**

invites you to toast the good times with favorites from America's most famous drinking establishments. We know you'll enjoy Playboy's selection of beverages from the premier taverns, saloons, pubs, and bars in this collection of

**DRINK RECIPES FROM 100 OF THE GREATEST BARS.**

Recipes selected and edited by
Playboy Clubs International

Photography by Dick Krueger

Produced for Philip Morris Incorporated
by Playboy Clubs International

The photographs in this book are designed
to provide ideas for serving the recipes in
your home and do not necessarily represent
the way the drinks are served in the
various establishments.

Recipes for the drinks that appear on the
front and back covers are included in
the book.

Published by
Philip Morris Incorporated
for Benson & Hedges 100's
100 Park Avenue
New York, New York 10017

Printed in the United States of America

## FOREWORD

Benson & Hedges 100's has published a series of unique volumes dedicated to good food and fine dining over the last three years.

The first two volumes, *100 of the World's Greatest Recipes,* were edited by our good friends Craig Claiborne and James Beard. Last year we selected 100 of America's greatest restaurants and persuaded their chefs to share their most prized recipes. The result was the third volume—*100 Recipes from 100 of the Greatest Restaurants.*

In looking back over this remarkable collection of 300 recipes, we decided that this year it was time to explore yet another side of good living and gracious entertaining.

We and our colleagues, the experts at Playboy, selected 100 of America's greatest bars for inclusion in this unique volume. Leading bartenders throughout the country have revealed the secrets of their most magnificent and renowned drink specialties.

You'll come upon delicious variations to dress up standard drinks, exotic specialties, and rare regional mixtures. All recipes have been carefully tested by Playboy for easy preparation, and include the information you need to mix and serve these drinks in your home.

Browse through the following pages. Discover what makes Buena Vista's Irish Coffee, in San Francisco, different from all other Irish coffees. Learn what secret gives the Bayou Swizzle from Sazerac's Bar, in New Orleans, its extra dash. Find out why the Marina Bay Club, in Fort Lauderdale, makes a Cherry Bomb Fireworks that people travel a hundred miles to sip.

Here's to your enjoyment of our latest volume, *Drink Recipes from 100 of the Greatest Bars.*

## Cheers!

# CONTENTS

# THE ALTA MIRA BAR

Sausalito, California

## Alta Mira Special Ramos Fizz

1½  ozs. gin or vodka
 ½  oz. orange curaçao
 3  ozs. half-and-half cream
    Juice of ½ lemon
 1  egg white
 2  teaspoons superfine sugar
 3  drops orange-flower water
    Ground nutmeg

Place all ingredients, except nutmeg, with ¼ cup crushed ice in blender. Blend until smooth. Strain into tall glass. Garnish with nutmeg.

*Yield: 1 serving*

## Coffee Alta Mira

1½  ozs. orange cognac brandy
    Black coffee, hot
    Whipped cream

Pour brandy into 6-oz. wineglass. Fill glass with coffee. Stir well. Top with a swirl of whipped cream. *Note*: To avoid possible breakage of the glass, pour the hot liquid over a metal spoon in the glass.

*Yield: 1 serving*

## Annie's Piña Colada

1⅛ ozs. rum
1 oz. crème de coconut
3 ozs. pineapple juice
1 oz. soft vanilla ice cream
1 pineapple chunk
1 maraschino cherry

Place all ingredients, except pineapple chunk and cherry, with crushed ice in blender. Blend until smooth. Pour into 13-oz. glass. Garnish with pineapple and cherry.

*Yield: 1 serving*

## Frozen Strawberry Margarita

1¼ ozs. gold tequila
½ oz. triple sec
1 oz. fresh lemon juice *or*
 ½ oz. fresh lime juice
4 ozs. frozen strawberries in sugar
 and juice, thawed
1 fresh strawberry, whole

Place all ingredients, except whole strawberry, with 1 handful of crushed ice in blender. Blend until almost frozen. Pour into 13-oz. glass. Garnish with whole strawberry.

*Yield: 1 serving*

## Banana Tree

1 oz. crème de bananes
$\frac{1}{2}$ oz. white crème de cacao
$\frac{1}{2}$ oz. Galliano
$\frac{1}{2}$ banana, sliced and peeled
6 ozs. vanilla ice cream
4 drops vanilla extract
1 banana slice, with skin
2 ozs. pineapple juice

Place all ingredients, except banana slice with skin and pineapple juice, in blender. Blend until thick and creamy. Pour into 14-oz. wineglass. Garnish with banana slice dipped in pineapple juice.

*Yield: 1 serving*

## Hot Peppermint Pattie

$1\frac{1}{4}$ ozs. peppermint schnapps
$\frac{3}{4}$ oz. dark crème de cacao
1 packet instant hot chocolate mix
Whipped cream
1 teaspoon green crème de menthe

Heat 16-oz. brandy snifter or coffee mug. Pour in schnapps and crème de cacao. Stir until mixed. Add packet of hot chocolate mix. Stir until dissolved. Fill to near top with boiling water. Top with swirl of whipped cream. Pour crème de menthe over whipped cream. *Note*: To avoid possible breakage of the glass brandy snifter, pour the hot liquid over a metal spoon in the glass.

*Yield: 1 serving*

## Hummer

1½ ozs. Mexican coffee liqueur
1 oz. light rum
8 ozs. vanilla ice cream
1 teaspoon sweet *or* bittersweet chocolate, shaved

Place all ingredients, except chocolate shavings, in blender. Blend until thick and smooth. Pour into 16-oz. glass. Garnish with chocolate shavings.

*Yield: 1 serving*

## Manfred's Sour Nail

1½ ozs. Scotch
½ oz. Scotch liqueur
3 ozs. orange juice
Juice of ½ lemon
Dash grenadine
Dash bar foam mix
Sugar (to taste)
1 orange slice
1 maraschino cherry

Place all ingredients, except orange slice and cherry, with 4 ozs. crushed ice in blender. Blend until smooth. Pour into chilled tall 12-oz. glass. Garnish with orange slice and cherry.

*Yield: 1 serving*

## Café Freeze

1½  ozs. rum
  8  ozs. lime sherbet
  3  ozs. pineapple juice

Place all ingredients in blender. Blend until smooth. Pour into tall 13-oz. glass.

*Yield: 1 serving*

## Peach Treat

2  ozs. peach-flavored brandy
2  ozs. orange juice
4  ozs. champagne, chilled
1  peach slice

Pour brandy and orange juice into blender. Blend until smooth. Pour into tall 13-oz. glass. Add champagne. Garnish with peach slice.

*Yield: 1 serving*

## Ice Palace

  1  oz. rum
½  oz. Galliano
½  oz. apricot-flavored brandy
  2  ozs. pineapple juice
¼  oz. lemon juice
  1  orange section
  1  maraschino cherry

Pour all ingredients, except orange section and cherry, over crushed ice in blender. Blend until smooth. Strain into tall 13-oz. glass. Garnish with orange section and cherry.

*Yield: 1 serving*   **7**

## Uncle Bob's Daiquiri

$1\frac{1}{2}$ ozs. Puerto Rican rum
$\frac{3}{4}$ oz. triple sec
$1\frac{1}{2}$ ozs. half-and-half cream
1 oz. whipping cream (optional)
$\frac{3}{4}$ oz. prepared sweet-and-sour mix
3 teaspoons frozen strawberries, thawed
1 orange slice

Place all ingredients, except orange slice, over ice in blender. Blend until smooth. Pour into chilled 13-oz. wineglass. Garnish with orange slice.

*Yield: 1 serving*

## California Root Beer Float

1 oz. Galliano
1 oz. Mexican coffee liqueur
3 ozs. half-and-half cream
1 oz. club soda

Pour all ingredients, except club soda, over ice in blender. Blend until smooth. Strain into 7-oz. wineglass. Top with club soda.

*Yield: 1 serving*

# BANANAS!

## Strawberry Banana Split

1½   ozs. banana liqueur
¾   oz. dark rum
4   ozs. frozen strawberries, thawed
½   banana, peeled and cut into slices
1½   ozs. half-and-half cream
1   teaspoon vanilla extract
1   fresh strawberry, whole
    Whipped cream

Place all ingredients, except 1 banana slice, whole strawberry, and whipped cream, with 3 ozs. crushed ice in blender. Blend until smooth and creamy. Pour into 17-oz. wineglass. Garnish with a swirl of whipped cream, the remaining banana slice, and the whole strawberry.

*Yield: 1 serving*

## Lola Granola

1½   ozs. amaretto liqueur
3   ozs. orange juice
1   oz. half-and-half cream
½   banana, peeled, cut into slices
½   teaspoon wheat germ

Place all ingredients, except wheat germ, with 4 ozs. crushed ice in blender. Blend until smooth and creamy. Pour into 17-oz. wineglass. Garnish with wheat germ.

*Yield: 1 serving*

## Pirate Grog

1½ ozs. light rum
½ oz. apricot-flavored brandy
½ oz. Falernum
2 ozs. prepared sweet-and-sour mix
1 oz. orange juice
2 dashes Angostura bitters
½ oz. dark rum
1 green cocktail cherry
1 maraschino cherry
1 pineapple chunk

Pour all ingredients, except dark rum, cherries, and pineapple, over ice in cocktail shaker. Shake well. Pour into tall 12-oz. glass. Float dark rum on drink. Garnish with cherries and pineapple chunk.

*Yield: 1 serving*

## Yellow Strawberry

1½ ozs. light rum
¾ oz. crème de bananes
2 ozs. frozen strawberries, thawed
1 oz. prepared sweet-and-sour mix
1 banana slice

Place all ingredients, except banana slice, with crushed ice in blender. Blend until smooth. Pour into 12-oz. brandy snifter. Put banana slice on rim of glass.

*Yield: 1 serving*

11

## Surber's Revenge

1½  ozs. light rum
    Juice of ½ lime
1   teaspoon honey
    Champagne, chilled

Pour all ingredients, except champagne, over crushed ice in cocktail shaker. Shake well. Strain into tall 8-oz. glass. Fill glass with champagne. Stir slightly.

*Yield: 1 serving*

## Bower's Excursion

1   oz. gin
1   oz. sweet vermouth
5   dashes curaçao
1   lemon peel strip
1   orange peel strip

Pour all ingredients, except lemon and orange strips, over ice cubes in cocktail shaker. Shake well. Strain into cocktail glass. Twist lemon and orange peels above drink and drop into glass.

*Yield: 1 serving*

## Howard's Surprise

2   ozs. vodka
1   oz. triple sec
    Dash Angostura bitters

Pour all ingredients over ice cubes in cocktail shaker. Shake well. Strain into cocktail glass.

*Yield: 1 serving*

# BlueBoarInn

San Francisco, California

## Blue Boar Nun

1   tablespoon dry cocoa mix
1   oz. black coffee, chilled
2   ozs. half-and-half cream
1   oz. Mexican coffee liqueur
1   Italian cookie

Place dry cocoa in saucepan. Add coffee and stir. Add half-and-half cream. Heat but do not boil. Add liqueur. Stir well. Pour into 5-oz. glass. Serve with cookie. *Note*: To avoid possible breakage of the glass, pour the hot liquid over a metal spoon in the glass.

*Yield: 1 serving*

## French Coffee

1   tablespoon sugar
1   oz. brandy
4   ozs. coffee, chilled
2   ozs. whipping cream
1   Italian cookie

Place sugar in saucepan. Add brandy. Stir well. Add coffee. Heat but do not boil. Pour into 8-oz. glass. Top with cream. Serve with cookie. *Note*: To avoid possible breakage of the glass, pour the hot liquid over a metal spoon in the glass.

*Yield: 1 serving*

## Malibu Wave

- 1 oz. tequila
- ½ oz. triple sec
- ⅛ oz. blue curacao
- 3 ozs. prepared sweet-and-sour mix
- 1 lime slice

Pour all ingredients, except lime slice, into blender. Fill blender with ice cubes. Blend until smooth. Pour into 14-oz. glass. Garnish with lime slice.

*Yield: 1 serving*

## Silver Cloud

- ¾ oz. amaretto liqueur
- ¾ oz. white crème de cacao
- 8 ozs. soft vanilla ice cream or
  1½ ozs. whipping cream
- ⅛ oz. coffee liqueur
  Whipped cream

Place all ingredients, except coffee liqueur and whipped cream, in blender. Fill blender ¾ full with ice cubes. Blend until smooth. Pour into 14-oz. glass. Swirl whipped cream on top. Drizzle coffee liqueur over whipped cream.

*Yield: 1 serving*

## Blue Barrel

    2  ozs. tequila
    1  oz. blue curaçao
 2½  ozs. prepared sweet-and-sour mix
    2  lime slices

Pour all ingredients, except lime slices, into 18-oz. wineglass with salted rim (dip moistened rim in salt). Fill with crushed ice. Stir well. Garnish with lime slices.

*Yield: 1 serving*

## Brewer's Nun

 2  ozs. gin
 2  ozs. triple sec
 2  ozs. lime juice
 2  maraschino cherries

Pour all ingredients, except cherries, into 18-oz. wineglass. Fill with ice. Stir well. Garnish with cherries.

*Yield: 1 serving*

## Brewer's Racker

 2  ozs. tequila
 5  ozs. iced tea
    Sugar (optional)
 1  lemon wedge
 1  lime slice

Pour tequila and iced tea into chilled tall 13-oz. glass. Fill with ice cubes. Add sugar to taste. Stir well. Garnish with lemon wedge and lime slice.

*Yield: 1 serving*

# BRICKSKELLER
## SALOON

## Bricklayer

| | |
|---|---|
| 1 | oz. white rum |
| 1 | oz. dark rum |
| ½ | oz. 151-proof rum |
| 1 | oz. grenadine |
| 1½ | ozs. orange juice |
| ½ | oz. 190-proof grain alcohol |
| 1 | orange wedge |
| 1 | lime wedge |

Pour all ingredients, except grain alcohol and fruit wedges, over ice cubes in cocktail shaker. Shake well. Strain over crushed ice in tall glass. Float grain alcohol. Garnish with fruit wedges.

*Yield: 1 serving*

## Outstanding Alexander

| | |
|---|---|
| 3 | ozs. vanilla ice cream |
| 3 | ozs. chocolate ice cream |
| 2 | ozs. whipping cream |
| 1½ | ozs. cognac |
| ½ | oz. Mexican coffee liqueur |
| ½ | oz. orange cognac brandy |
| | Ground nutmeg |

Place ice creams and cream with ½ cup crushed ice in blender. Blend until creamy. Add cognac, coffee liqueur, and brandy. Blend until smooth. Pour into 2 large wineglasses. Garnish with nutmeg.

*Yield: 2 servings*

# Buena vista

## Irish Coffee

      3   cocktail sugar cubes
          Black coffee, hot
  1¼    ozs. Irish whiskey
          Whipped cream

Place sugar cubes in warmed 6-oz. glass. Fill glass ¾ full with coffee. Stir until sugar is dissolved. Add whiskey. Stir well. Top with swirl of whipped cream. *Note*: To avoid possible breakage of the glass, pour the hot liquid over a metal spoon in the glass.

*Yield: 1 serving*

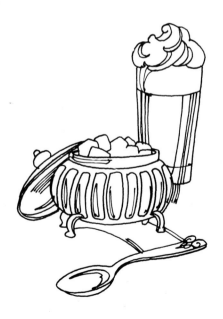

# BULL & BUSH

## Strawberry Slush

    4   ozs. cracked ice
    2   to 3 ozs. fresh strawberries or
        frozen strawberries, thawed
1½     ozs. crème de noyaux
    1   oz. passion-fruit syrup
    2   ozs. half-and-half cream
    1   strawberry, whole
        Whipped cream

Place all ingredients, except whole strawberry and whipped cream, in blender. Blend until slushy. Pour into 14-oz. wineglass. Top with swirl of whipped cream. Garnish with strawberry.

*Yield: 1 serving*

# Bully III

Vail, Colorado

## Jack's Casting Couch

1   oz. crème de almond
1   oz. crème de cacao
4   ozs. vanilla ice cream

Place all ingredients with ½ cup crushed ice in blender. Blend well. Pour into 18-oz. wineglass.

*Yield: 1 serving*

Chicago, Illinois

## Harvey Wallbanger

1   oz. vodka
½   oz. Galliano
6   ozs. orange juice

Pour all ingredients over 1 heaping table-spoon crushed ice in blender. Blend well. Strain over ice cubes in 10-oz. glass mug.

*Yield: 1 serving*

# CARGO BAR

Mission Bay, California

## Maui Christmas

1½   ozs. triple sec
1   oz. white crème de cacao
3½   ozs. pineapple juice
1   tablespoon coconut snow
1   maraschino cherry

Place all ingredients, except cherry, with crushed ice in blender. Blend well. Pour into tall glass. Garnish with cherry.

*Yield: 1 serving*

21

## Charlie's Freeze

¾ oz. Mexican coffee liqueur
¾ oz. California brandy
5 ozs. vanilla ice cream
  Whipped cream
  Ground nutmeg

Place all ingredients, except whipped cream and nutmeg, in blender. Blend until thick. Pour into 9-oz. wineglass. Top with swirl of whipped cream. Garnish with nutmeg.

*Yield: 1 serving*

## Spanish Martini

1½ ozs. dry gin
½ oz. dry Spanish sherry
1 green olive or lemon peel strip

Pour gin and sherry over ice cubes in cocktail shaker. Stir 20 times. Strain into chilled cocktail glass. Add either the olive or twist the lemon peel above drink and drop into glass.

*Yield: 1 serving*

## Tica

1   oz. Tuaca
1   oz. Jamaican coffee liqueur
1   oz. whipping cream

Pour all ingredients over ice cubes in old-fashioned glass. Stir well.

*Yield: 1 serving*

## Irish Spring

1   oz. Irish whiskey
³/₄  oz. peach brandy
1   oz. orange juice
1   oz. prepared sweet-and-sour mix
1   orange slice
1   maraschino cherry

Pour all ingredients, except orange slice and cherry, over crushed ice in 10-oz. chimney glass. Stir well. Garnish with orange slice and cherry.

*Yield: 1 serving*

![Charley Magruder's logo — bowler hat]

# Charley Magruder's

Atlanta, Georgia

## Jelly Bean

1½  ozs. Southern Comfort
 ½  oz. grenadine
 ½  oz. 151-proof rum

Pour Southern Comfort and grenadine over ice cubes in old-fashioned glass. Stir well. Float rum on drink.

*Yield: 1 serving*

## Georgia Bulldog

1  oz. tequila
½  oz. Mexican coffee liqueur
1  oz. whipping cream
   Cola, chilled

Pour all ingredients, except cola, over ice cubes in 10-oz. wineglass. Stir well. Top with cola.

*Yield: 1 serving*

## Irish Gremlin

$3/4$  oz. Irish whiskey
$3/4$  oz. vodka
 2  ozs. orange juice
    Ginger ale, chilled
    Dash grenadine
$2\frac{1}{2}$  orange slices

Pour whiskey, vodka, and orange juice over ice cubes in tall 10-oz. glass. Stir well. Fill glass with ginger ale. Stir in grenadine. Garnish with orange slices.

*Yield: 1 serving*

## Emerald Isle Cooler

6  ozs. vanilla ice cream
1  oz. crème de menthe
1  oz. Irish whiskey
   Club soda, chilled

Place ice cream in tall 14-oz. glass. Add crème de menthe and whiskey. Stir well. Fill glass with club soda. Stir well.

*Yield: 1 serving*

# Clarence Foster's

Atlanta, Georgia

## Egbert

2   ozs. vodka or rum
1   raw egg
1   teaspoon frozen concentrated orange juice
1   fresh orange, peeled and sectioned
    Dash sugar
    Dash club soda
    Dash lemon juice
1   lemon slice

Place all ingredients, except lemon slice, with ice in blender. Blend well. Pour into tall 8-oz. glass. Garnish with lemon slice.

*Yield: 1 serving*

## Foster's Banana

1¼   ozs. vodka
 ½   oz. Cherry Heering
     Pineapple juice
 ½   fresh banana, split lengthwise and peeled

Pour vodka and Cherry Heering over ice cubes in tall 12-oz. glass. Stir until mixed. Fill glass with pineapple juice. Stir well. Garnish with banana.

*Yield: 1 serving*

**27**

## Hollywood Hot

1½  ozs. orange cognac brandy
 7  ozs. tea, hot
 1  orange slice

Pour brandy into 12-oz. brandy snifter. Add hot tea. Stir well. Garnish with orange slice. *Note*: To avoid possible breakage of the brandy snifter, pour the hot liquid over a metal spoon in the snifter.

*Yield: 1 serving*


## May Punch

6  ozs. imported May wine, chilled
6  ozs. brut champagne, chilled
1  brandied strawberry*

Pour May wine and champagne into chilled 14-oz. wineglass. Garnish with strawberry.
  \* **Brandied Strawberry**: Soak fresh strawberry in brandy ½ hour.

*Yield: 1 serving*

# THE COLORADO MINE COMPANY

Denver, Colorado

## The Zamboanga Hummer

| | |
|---|---|
| $3/4$ | oz. gold rum |
| $3/4$ | oz. gin |
| $3/4$ | oz. brandy |
| $3/4$ | oz. orange curaçao |
| 2 | ozs. fresh orange juice, chilled |
| 2 | ozs. fresh pineapple juice, chilled |
| $1/2$ | oz. fresh lemon juice, chilled |
| 1 | teaspoon brown sugar |

Pour all ingredients over $1/2$ cup crushed ice in blender. Blend until smooth. Pour into tall 14-oz. glass.

*Yield: 1 serving*

## The Coming and Going

| | |
|---|---|
| $1 1/2$ | ozs. Greek brandy |
| 4 | ozs. prune juice, chilled |

Pour ingredients into strong paper cup. Stir well.

*Yield: 1 serving*

## Cowcatcher

1 oz. cognac
1 oz. amaretto liqueur

Pour ingredients into brandy snifter ¾ full of crushed ice. Stir well.

*Yield: 1 serving*

## Lil' Red Caboose

1 oz. brandy
½ oz. triple sec
½ oz. grenadine
6 ozs. fruit punch, chilled
1 orange slice

Pour all ingredients, except orange slice, over crushed ice in cocktail shaker. Shake well. Strain over ice cubes in brandy snifter. Garnish with orange slice.

*Yield: 1 serving*

## The Cricket

    4    ozs. white wine, chilled
    1    oz. vodka
    ½    oz. blue curaçao
    1    orange slice

Pour all ingredients, except orange slice, into 6-oz. wineglass. Stir well. Garnish with orange slice.

*Yield: 1 serving*

## Big Apple

    1    oz. vodka
    ½    oz. amaretto liqueur
    4    ozs. apple juice, chilled
         Club soda
    1    apple wedge

Pour all ingredients, except club soda and apple wedge, over ice cubes in tall 8-oz. glass. Stir well. Top with club soda. Garnish with apple wedge.

*Yield: 1 serving*

San Francisco, California

## Crisis Cocktail

1 oz. gin
1 oz. vodka
1 oz. apricot-flavored brandy
3 ozs. champagne, chilled
3 ozs. ginger ale, chilled
1 orange slice
1 maraschino cherry

Pour gin, vodka, and brandy over ice cubes in 18-oz. wineglass. Add champagne and ginger ale. Stir very slightly. Garnish with orange slice and cherry.

*Yield: 1 serving*

## Bag Dad By The Bay

1¼ ozs. dark rum
1¼ ozs. Galliano
5 ozs. fresh orange juice, chilled
1 orange slice
1 lime slice

Pour rum and Galliano over ice cubes in tulip champagne glass. Add orange juice. Stir well. Garnish with orange and lime slices.

*Yield: 1 serving*

## Cye's Moustache

½  oz. crème de noyaux
½  oz. banana liqueur
½  oz. whipping cream

To float ingredients in layers, slowly pour them in the order listed into a 2-oz. pony glass.

*Yield: 1 serving*

## Cye's Coffee

1  teaspoon brown sugar
8  ozs. black coffee, hot
¾  oz. orange cognac brandy
¾  oz. 6-year-old dark rum
   Whipped cream

Place brown sugar in tall 12-oz. glass. Add 2 ozs. of the coffee. Stir until sugar is dissolved. Add brandy, rum, and remaining coffee. Stir well. Top with swirl of whipped cream. *Note*: To avoid possible breakage of the glass, pour the hot liquid over a metal spoon in the glass.

*Yield: 1 serving*

## Daisy Buchanan

### Irish Brogue

$^3/_4$   oz. Irish whiskey liqueur
$^1/_2$   oz. Irish whiskey

Pour ingredients over ice cubes in cocktail shaker. Shake well. Strain over ice cubes in old-fashioned glass.

*Yield: 1 serving*

### Daisy Pardi

$^1/_2$   oz. triple sec
$^1/_2$   oz. cognac
$^1/_2$   oz. orange juice

Pour all ingredients over ice cubes in cocktail shaker. Shake well. Strain into cocktail glass.

*Yield: 1 serving*

## Dobson's Monkey

1   oz. crème de bananes
1   oz. crème de cacao (dark)
1   oz. whipping cream
    Unsweetened shredded coconut

Pour all ingredients, except coconut, over 3 ice cubes in cocktail shaker. Shake well. Strain into cocktail glass. Garnish with coconut.

*Yield: 1 serving*

## Toasted Almond Bar

1   oz. amaretto liqueur
1   oz. crème de cacao (light)
1   oz. whipping cream
1   teaspoon dark chocolate, shaved

Pour all ingredients, except chocolate shavings, over 3 ice cubes in cocktail shaker. Shake well. Strain into cocktail glass. Garnish with chocolate shavings.

*Yield: 1 serving*

## Colorado Road

1   oz. brandy
1   oz. crème de cacao (dark)
    Cola
1   lime wedge

Pour brandy and crème de cacao into cocktail shaker. Add 2 ozs. crushed ice. Shake well. Pour into 8-oz. glass. Add cola to fill. Garnish with lime wedge.

*Yield: 1 serving*

# DONOVAN'S ☘
## COPPER BAR

**Vail, Colorado**

## Snowshoe

$^3/_4$  oz. brandy
$^3/_4$  oz. white crème de menthe

Pour ingredients over ice in old-fashioned glass. Stir well.

*Yield: 1 serving*

## Kamikaze

1  oz. vodka
Dash bottled lime juice

Pour vodka over crushed ice to chill in cocktail shaker. Add dash of bottled lime juice. Strain into shot glass.

*Yield: 1 serving*

# DOWNEY'S

Philadelphia, Pennsylvania

## Downey's Orange Crème

1½ ozs. vodka
 1 teaspoon orange cognac brandy
   Juice of 2 oranges
 1 oz. half-and-half cream
 1 tablespoon superfine sugar
 1 orange slice

Place all ingredients, except orange slice, with 1 cup crushed ice in blender. Blend until frothy. Pour into 10-oz. wineglass. Garnish with orange slice.

*Yield: 1 serving*

## Sparkling Jack Apple

½ oz. apple liqueur
 4 to 6 ozs. champagne, chilled
 1 apple wedge

Pour apple liqueur into champagne glass. Add champagne. Float apple wedge for garnish.

*Yield: 1 serving*

## Fogcutter

$^3/_4$   oz. brandy
$^3/_4$   oz. rum
$^1/_2$   oz. gin
  3   ozs. pineapple juice
  1   oz. prepared sweet-and-sour mix
  1   lime wedge
  1   lemon wedge

Pour all ingredients, except lemon and lime wedges, over ice in cocktail shaker. Shake well. Strain into tall 12-oz. glass. Squeeze lemon and lime wedges above drink and drop into glass.

*Yield: 1 serving*

## Bubble Gum

$^1/_2$   oz. blackberry-flavored brandy
  3   ozs. orange juice
  1   oz. whipping cream
$^1/_2$   oz. grenadine
  1   gum ball *or* jawbreaker

Pour all ingredients, except gum ball, over ice in cocktail shaker. Shake well. Strain into tall 8-oz. glass. Drop gum ball into drink.

*Yield: 1 serving*

## Grease Job

1¼    ozs. vodka
1¼    ozs. almond liqueur
1¼    ozs. cherry-flavored brandy
  5    ozs. pineapple juice
  3    ozs. orange juice
  1    lime wheel
        Sugar
        Splash grain alcohol

Pour all ingredients, except lime slice, sugar, and grain alcohol, into blender. Blend thoroughly. Pour over ice cubes in 22-oz. glass. Sprinkle lime wheel with sugar and float on drink. Add splash of grain alcohol. Serve flaming.

*Yield: 1 serving*


## Anti-Freeze

  1    package (1 oz.) hot chocolate mix
1¼    ozs. peppermint schnapps
  6    ozs. boiling water
        Whipped cream
  1    maraschino cherry
  1    peppermint stick

Pour hot chocolate mix into 9-oz. glass mug. Add schnapps and boiling water. Stir well. Top with swirl of whipped cream. Garnish with cherry and peppermint stick. *Note*: To avoid possible breakage of the glass mug, pour the hot liquid over a metal spoon in the mug.

*Yield: 1 serving*

## Anvil

2   ozs. vodka
4   ozs. coconut milk
3   tablespoons crushed pineapple
    Ground nutmeg

Place all ingredients, except nutmeg, with 2 cups crushed ice in blender. Blend until frothy. Strain into chilled tall 12-oz. glass. Garnish with nutmeg.

*Yield: 1 serving*

## Forge Special

$3/4$   oz. blended whiskey
$3/4$   oz. rum
1   oz. passion-fruit syrup
1   oz. lemon juice

Pour all ingredients over 2 cups crushed ice in blender. Blend until frothy. Strain into chilled champagne glass.

*Yield: 1 serving*

43

# THE FOUR SEASONS

## The Four Seasons' Strawberry Summer Cooler

1½ ozs. apricot-flavored brandy
1 cup strawberries
2 ozs. grapefruit juice
2 ozs. pineapple juice
2 ozs. orange juice
1 teaspoon superfine sugar
1 strawberry, whole

Place all ingredients, except whole strawberry, with ½ cup crushed ice in blender. Blend until smooth. Pour into tall 14-oz. glass. Garnish with strawberry.

*Yield: 1 serving*

## Viennese Hussar

1½ ozs. apricot-flavored brandy
1½ ozs. tonic water
1 lemon peel strip

Pour brandy and tonic water into old-fashioned glass. Stir. Twist lemon peel above drink and drop into glass.

*Yield: 1 serving*

**45**

# Fran O'Brien's

## Volga Boatman

1½ ozs. vodka
1½ ozs. apricot liqueur
5 ozs. lemon juice
1 orange slice
1 maraschino cherry

Pour all ingredients, except orange slice and cherry, over crushed ice in cocktail shaker. Shake well. Pour into tall 12-oz. glass. Garnish with orange slice and cherry.

*Yield: 1 serving*

## Fran's-Sicle

6 ozs. orange juice, chilled
1 oz. Mexican coffee liqueur
1 oz. whipping cream

Pour all ingredients over crushed ice in cocktail shaker. Shake well. Strain into tall 8-oz. glass.

*Yield: 1 serving*

Memphis, Tennessee

## Gorilla Punch

1   oz. vodka
½   oz. blue curaçao
2   ozs. orange juice
2   ozs. pineapple juice
1   maraschino cherry

Pour all ingredients, except cherry, over ice in cocktail shaker. Shake well. Strain over ice cubes in tall 12-oz. glass. Garnish with cherry.

*Yield: 1 serving*

## Bob Cratchit's Cup

1   oz. coffee liqueur
¾   oz. white crème de menthe
    Black coffee, hot
    Whipped cream
1   teaspoon sweet chocolate, shaved

Pour liqueur and crème de menthe into coffee mug. Add hot coffee up to 1 inch from rim. Stir well. Top with swirl of whipped cream. Garnish with chocolate shavings.

*Yield: 1 serving*

# HARRISON'S
## *on Peachtree*

## Traffic Light

$\frac{1}{2}$   oz. grenadine
$\frac{1}{2}$   oz. crème de menthe
$\frac{1}{2}$   oz. peppermint schnapps
$\frac{1}{2}$   oz. Galliano

To float the ingredients in layers, slowly pour them in the order listed into 2-oz. liqueur glass.

*Yield: 1 serving*

## Morning After

2   ozs. crème de cacao or Mexican coffee liqueur
6   ozs. vanilla ice cream
1   egg
2   ozs. half-and-half cream
    Ground nutmeg

Place all ingredients, except nutmeg, in blender. Blend until thick. Pour into tall 12-oz. glass. Garnish with nutmeg.

*Yield: 1 serving*

## Peachtree Cooler

5   ozs. Chablis, chilled
$\frac{1}{4}$   oz. crème de cassis
$1\frac{1}{2}$   ozs. club soda
1   lemon peel strip or lime wedge

Pour Chablis over ice cubes in 12-oz. glass. Add crème de cassis and club soda. Stir slightly. Twist lemon peel or squeeze lime wedge above drink and drop into glass.

*Yield: 1 serving*

# Hasenour's

Louisville, Kentucky

## Brave Bull

1 oz. tequila
½ oz. Mexican coffee liqueur

Pour tequila and coffee liqueur over cracked ice in old-fashioned glass. Stir well.

*Yield: 1 serving*

## Mint Julep

6 mint leaves
½ oz. simple syrup mix*
2 ozs. bourbon
1 mint sprig

Place 6 mint leaves in tall 12-oz. glass. Add simple syrup mix. Muddle mint leaves. Add 1 oz. bourbon. Fill glass with crushed ice. Add remaining bourbon. Stir thoroughly. Garnish with mint sprig.
  * **Simple Syrup Mix:** Place 4 teaspoons granulated sugar and ½ oz. water in saucepan. Cook until sugar dissolves, stirring occasionally.

*Yield: 1 serving*

## Gin Buck

1 oz. gin
2 ozs. orange juice
  Ginger ale, chilled
1 lime wedge
1 maraschino cherry

Pour gin and orange juice over ice cubes in 12-oz. glass. Fill glass with ginger ale. Stir well. Squeeze lime wedge above drink and drop into glass. Garnish with cherry.

**50**

*Yield: 1 serving*

## Tequila Sunrise

1½ ozs. tequila
3 ozs. orange juice, chilled
½ oz. grenadine
1 lime wedge
1 maraschino cherry

Pour tequila and orange juice over crushed ice in 13-oz. glass. Stir well. Add grenadine and stir. Garnish with lime wedge and cherry.

*Yield: 1 serving*

## Houlihan's Sangría

½ gallon red Burgundy, chilled
1 quart grapefruit juice, chilled
½ gallon orange juice, chilled
½ gallon simple syrup mix,* chilled
  Champagne, chilled
20 grapefruit or orange slices
20 lime wedges or mint sprigs

Pour Burgundy, grapefruit and orange juices, and simple syrup mix into large bowl. Mix well. Pour over ice cubes in 20-oz. glasses. Top each glass with 1½ ozs. champagne. Garnish each drink with grapefruit or orange slices, and with lime wedge or mint sprig.

* **Simple Syrup Mix:** Place 8 cups granulated sugar and 8 cups water in pan. Cook until sugar dissolves, stirring occasionally.

*Yield: 20 servings*

# Jimmy's Milan

## Jill's Stinger

¾ oz. Jamaican coffee liqueur
¼ oz. white crème de menthe
¼ oz. sweet vermouth

Pour coffee liqueur over crushed ice in old-fashioned glass. Add crème de menthe. Stir slightly. Float sweet vermouth on drink.

*Yield: 1 serving*

## Sunbeam

1½ ozs. Galliano
¾ oz. sweet vermouth

Pour Galliano over crushed ice in old-fashioned glass. Float vermouth on drink.

*Yield: 1 serving*

# LANDMARK TAVERN

## Irish Tea

1½  ozs. orange cognac brandy
 4  to 5 ozs. tea, hot
 ½  teaspoon sugar
    Whipped cream
 1  large orange peel strip

Pour brandy into 8-oz. glass mug. Add tea and sugar. Stir. Top with swirl of whipped cream. Twist orange peel above drink and drop into mug. *Note*: To avoid possible breakage of the glass mug, pour the hot liquid over a metal spoon in the mug.

*Yield: 1 serving*

## Hot Buttered Rum

¼  pound lightly salted butter
 6  tablespoons brown sugar
 1  tablespoon mace
 1  tablespoon allspice
 2  teaspoons crushed cloves
    Dark Jamaican rum
    Boiling water
    Ground nutmeg

Cream butter, brown sugar, mace, allspice, and cloves until smooth. Place 1 tablespoon of batter into each 8-oz. glass mug. Add 1½ ozs. rum and 4 ozs. boiling water to each mug. Stir until smooth. Add more batter if desired. Garnish with nutmeg. *Note*: To avoid possible breakage of the glass mug, pour the hot liquid over a metal spoon in the mug.

*Yield: 6 to 8 servings*

Le Central

Perroquet

# Le Central

## Perroquet

1   oz. Pernod
½   oz. green crème de menthe

Pour ingredients over ice cubes in old-fashioned glass. Stir well.

*Yield: 1 serving*


## Chamonix

1   oz. crème de cassis
5   ozs. red Burgundy, chilled

Pour crème de cassis over a few ice cubes in 8-oz. wineglass. Add Burgundy. Stir well.

*Yield: 1 serving*

# *Lettuce*

## Lettuceade

1¼  ozs. vodka
 8  ozs. orange sherbet
 1  oz. orange juice
    Whipped cream
 1  maraschino cherry

Place all ingredients, except whipped cream and cherry, with ½ cup crushed ice in blender. Blend until slushy. Pour into 17-oz. brandy snifter. Top with swirl of whipped cream. Garnish with cherry.

*Yield: 1 serving*

## Chocolate Snow Bear

1¼  ozs. amaretto liqueur
 1  oz. crème de cacao
 8  ozs. French vanilla ice cream
 ¼  oz. chocolate syrup
 2  dashes vanilla extract

Place all ingredients with ½ cup crushed ice in blender. Blend until thick and creamy. Pour into 17-oz. brandy snifter.

*Yield: 1 serving*

## The Lift Cooler

¼  oz. triple sec
½  oz. orange juice
½  oz. prepared sweet-and-sour mix
6  oz. red wine
    Club soda

Pour triple sec, orange juice, and sweet-and-sour mix over ice cubes in 12-oz. wineglass. Stir well. Add red wine. Stir well. Splash with club soda.

*Yield: 1 serving*

## Spanish Coffee

1    teaspoon granulated sugar
½   oz. 151-proof rum
1¼  ozs. Mexican coffee liqueur
     Black coffee, hot
     Whipped cream
¼   oz. Cherry Heering

Dip moistened rim of 8-oz. wineglass into sugar. Pour rum into glass. Ignite rum and twist glass to caramelize sugar. Pour liqueur into glass. Fill with hot coffee. Stir well. Top with swirl of whipped cream. Drizzle Cherry Heering over whipped cream. *Note*: To avoid possible breakage of the glass, pour the hot liquid over a metal spoon in the glass.

*Yield: 1 serving*

## THE LION BAR

Chicago, Illinois

### Lion Tamer

1¼ ozs. Southern Comfort
¼ oz. apple liqueur
¾ oz. lemon juice
Dash grenadine

Pour all ingredients into blender. Blend thoroughly. Pour into old-fashioned glass.

*Yield: 1 serving*

### Lioness

1 oz. amaretto liqueur
½ oz. triple sec
1 oz. whipping cream

Pour all ingredients into blender. Blend thoroughly. Pour into cocktail glass.

*Yield: 1 serving*

Denver, Colorado

## Hogan & Burns

1½  ozs. caramel liqueur
2  ozs. whipping cream
1  oz. orange juice
½  oz. club soda

Pour all ingredients into blender. Blend until thoroughly mixed. Pour over ice cubes in tall 12-oz. glass.

*Yield: 1 serving*

## McFlying Saucer

3/4  oz. Mexican coffee liqueur
3/4  oz. amaretto liqueur
 3   ozs. half-and-half cream
     Ground cinnamon

Pour all ingredients, except cinnamon, over 1/2 cup crushed ice in blender. Blend until smooth. Pour into 12-oz. tulip champagne glass. Garnish with cinnamon.

*Yield: 1 serving*

## Carmel Fog

 3   ozs. white wine
 3   ozs. pineapple chunks
 2   ozs. coconut flakes
 1   oz. orange juice
1/4  oz. half-and-half cream

Place all ingredients with 1/2 cup crushed ice in blender. Blend until smooth. Pour into 12-oz. tulip champagne glass.

*Yield: 1 serving*

San Antonio, Texas

## Italian Delight

1½  ozs. amaretto liqueur
3½  ozs. orange juice
2    ozs. half-and-half cream
1    maraschino cherry

Pour all ingredients, except cherry, over ice in cocktail shaker. Shake well. Strain over ice cubes in 12-oz. brandy snifter. Garnish with cherry.

*Yield: 1 serving*

## Velvet Hammer

6  ozs. French vanilla ice cream
1  oz. triple sec
1  oz. white crème de cacao

Place ice cream in blender. Add triple sec and crème de cacao. Blend until thick and smooth. Pour into 12-oz. brandy snifter.

*Yield: 1 serving*

## Kir

½  oz. crème de cassis
5  ozs. Drouhin Soleil Blanc, chilled

Pour crème de cassis into 12-oz. wineglass. Add wine. Stir slightly.

*Yield: 1 serving*

## Café Brûlot

Peel of 1 lemon, cut in 1 long spiral
Peel of 1 orange, cut in 1 long spiral
10  cloves
16  ozs. black coffee, hot
2  cinnamon sticks
10  sugar cubes
1½  ozs. orange cognac brandy
1½  ozs. brandy
6  lemon peel strips

Pierce each long lemon and orange peel with 5 cloves. Pierce and intertwine the peels on 1 fork, making sure they are secure. Pour coffee into flameproof bowl. Add cinnamon sticks. Place 5 sugar cubes in large ladle. Pour orange cognac brandy into ladle. Ignite orange cognac brandy and pour over peels on fork into coffee. Repeat procedure with remaining sugar cubes and the brandy. Place peels on fork in coffee; let stand 1 minute and remove. Pour 3 ozs. Café Brûlot into a demitasse. Twist lemon strip above drink and drop into cup. Repeat with remaining Café Brûlot and lemon peel strips.

*Yield: 6 servings*

Fort Lauderdale, Florida

## Cherry Bomb Fireworks

1  oz. vodka
1  oz. white rum
1  oz. tequila
6  ozs. piña colada mix, chilled
1  drop red food coloring
1  maraschino cherry

Pour all ingredients, except cherry, over ice cubes in tall 12-oz. glass. Stir slightly. Garnish with cherry.

*Yield: 1 serving*

## Marina Bay's Knuckle Punch

$3/4$  oz. brandy
$3/4$  oz. vodka
$1/2$  oz. triple sec
$1/2$  oz. white crème de menthe
$5^1/_2$  ozs. prepared sweet-and-sour mix, chilled
1  lemon or lime peel strip

Pour all ingredients, except lemon or lime strip, over crushed ice in tall 12-oz. glass. Stir slightly. Twist lemon or lime peel over drink and drop into glass.

*Yield: 1 serving*

# MARKET STREET EXCHANGE

Cleveland, Ohio

## Cherry Blizzard

1½   ozs. cherry-flavored brandy
     Club soda, chilled
1    lemon peel strip

Pour brandy over crushed ice in cocktail glass. Fill glass with club soda. Twist lemon peel above drink and drop into glass.

*Yield: 1 serving*


## Coconut Toastie

1½   ozs. dark rum
2    tablespoons vanilla ice cream
¼    oz. whipping cream
     Toasted shredded coconut

Place all ingredients, except coconut, in blender. Blend until smooth and creamy. Pour into champagne glass. Garnish with coconut.

*Yield: 1 serving*

65

## Avalanche

| | |
|---|---|
| 1 | oz. crème de bananes |
| 1/2 | oz. white crème de cacao |
| | Dash amaretto liqueur |
| 1 | oz. half-and-half cream |
| 1/2 | fresh banana, peeled |

Place all ingredients with crushed ice in blender. Blend to frappé texture. Pour into 14-oz. glass.

*Yield: 1 serving*

## Maude's Berry Bomb

| | |
|---|---|
| 1 1/2 | ozs. vodka |
| 1/2 | oz. cranberry liqueur |
| 1/2 | oz. grenadine |
| 1 | teaspoon granulated sugar |
| 1 | teaspoon whole cranberry sauce |
| 1 | oz. half-and-half cream |

Place all ingredients with crushed ice in blender. Blend to frappé texture. Pour into tall 14-oz. glass. Garnish with whole cranberry if desired.

*Yield: 1 serving*

# Maxwell's Plum

## Fresh Framboise Champagne

2 ozs. fresh raspberries
6 ozs. champagne, chilled
  Superfine sugar

Muddle the raspberries in cup. Spoon into chilled tulip champagne glass. Add champagne. Sweeten to taste with sugar.

*Yield: 1 serving*

## Fresh Mint Daiquiri

1¼ ozs. Puerto Rican rum
 ¾ oz. crème de menthe
1½ ozs. fresh lime juice
 1 tablespoon superfine sugar
 2 mint sprigs

Place all ingredients with ¼ cup crushed ice in blender. Blend thoroughly. Strain into chilled whiskey-sour glass.

*Yield: 1 serving*

# The Mews

Provincetown, Massachusetts

## Pear Cream

2 ozs. pear-flavored brandy
1 oz. pineapple juice
1 oz. whipping cream

Pour all ingredients over ice in cocktail shaker. Shake heartily. Strain into white wineglass.

*Yield: 1 serving*

## Georgianna

3 ozs. champagne, chilled
½ oz. vodka
½ oz. orange liqueur
Orange juice
1 orange wheel

Pour all ingredients, except orange juice and orange wheel, into fluted tulip glass. Stir slowly. Fill glass with orange juice. Garnish with orange wheel.

*Yield: 1 serving*

## Vermouth Cassis

3 ozs. dry French vermouth
½ oz. crème de cassis
½ orange slice
Club soda

Pour vermouth and crème de cassis over ice in 12-oz. highball glass. Stir well. Squeeze orange slice above drink and drop in glass. Top with club soda.

*Yield: 1 serving*

# the mill falls

Newton Upper Falls, Massachusetts

## Ginger Snap Cocktail

1½ ozs. light rum
½ oz. ginger-flavored brandy
    Gingersnap cookies

Pour rum and brandy over shaved ice in old-fashioned glass. Stir slightly. Serve with cookies.

*Yield: 1 serving*

## The Mill Falls Special

1 oz. amaretto liqueur
1 oz. vodka
1 teaspoon sambuca liqueur

Pour all ingredients over ice cubes in old-fashioned glass. Stir well.

*Yield: 1 serving*

Atlanta, Georgia

## Mimi's Peach Daiquiri

1 oz. rum
¾ oz. prepared sweet-and-sour mix
½ peach, sliced
1 peach wedge
1 maraschino cherry

Place all ingredients, except peach wedge and cherry, with ½ cup crushed ice in blender. Blend until smooth. Pour into large wineglass. Garnish with peach wedge and cherry.

*Yield: 1 serving*  **71**

# Mr. SMITH'S

## Ice in Heaven

- $3/4$ oz. Mexican coffee liqueur
- $1/4$ oz. crème de noyaux
- 2 ozs. half-and-half cream

Pour all ingredients over ice cubes in 12-oz. brandy snifter. Stir slightly.

*Yield: 1 serving*

## Iguana

- 1 oz. vodka
- 1 oz. tequila
- $3/4$ oz. Mexican coffee liqueur
- 3 ozs. sweetened lemon *or* lime juice
- 1 lime wedge

Pour all ingredients, except lime wedge, over crushed ice in cocktail shaker. Shake well. Pour into tall 14-oz. glass. Garnish with lime wedge.

*Yield: 1 serving*

# MRS. O'LEARY'S

Chicago, Illinois

## Gibson Girl

1 oz. anisette
1 oz. sweet vermouth
5 ozs. whipping cream
1 black licorice stick

Pour all ingredients, except licorice stick, over ice cubes in cocktail shaker. Shake well. Strain into whiskey-sour glass. Garnish with licorice stick.

*Yield: 1 serving*

## Pepper's Punch

1 oz. brandy
1 oz. amaretto liqueur
1 oz. crème de bananes
4 ozs. whipping cream
1 banana stick
　Ground nutmeg

Pour all ingredients, except banana stick and nutmeg, into blender. Blend well. Pour into punch glass. Garnish with banana stick and nutmeg.

*Yield: 1 serving*

73

# THE MUTINY

Coconut Grove, Florida

## Whoopsie Daisy

| | |
|---|---|
| 1¼ | ozs. tequila |
| ¼ | oz. banana liqueur |
| 2½ | ozs. orange juice |
| 1 | orange slice |

Pour all ingredients, except orange slice, into blender. Blend until smooth. Pour into champagne glass. Garnish with orange slice.

*Yield: 1 serving*

Beverly Hills, California

## Golden Eye

| | |
|---|---|
| 1¼ | ozs. vodka |
| ¾ | oz. triple sec |
| 2 | ozs. orange juice |
| ½ | oz. simple syrup mix* |
| 1 | egg yolk |
| 1 | orange slice |

Place all ingredients, except orange slice, with crushed ice in blender. Blend until smooth. Pour into 12-oz. brandy snifter. Garnish with orange slice.

**\* Simple Syrup Mix:** Place 4 teaspoons granulated sugar and ½ oz. water in saucepan. Cook until sugar dissolves, stirring occasionally.

*Yield: 1 serving*

# OakBar

## Atlantic Breeze

| | |
|---|---|
| 1 | oz. rum |
| ½ | oz. apricot-flavored brandy |
| 5 | ozs. pineapple juice |
| 1 | oz. lemon juice |
| | Dash of grenadine |
| ½ | oz. Galliano |
| 1 | orange slice |
| 1 | maraschino cherry |

Pour all ingredients, except Galliano, orange slice, and cherry, into tall 14-oz. glass half filled with crushed ice. Stir well. Top drink with Galliano. Garnish with orange slice and cherry.

*Yield: 1 serving*


## Troika Cocktail

| | |
|---|---|
| 1 | oz. vodka |
| ½ | oz. Mexican coffee liqueur |
| 1 | oz. lemon juice |

Pour all ingredients over ice cubes in cocktail shaker. Shake well. Strain into cocktail glass.

*Yield: 1 serving*

## Smith & Kearns

1½  ozs. Mexican coffee liqueur
3½  ozs. half-and-half cream
1½  ozs. club soda

Pour liqueur and cream over crushed ice in 10-oz. glass. Top drink with club soda.

*Yield: 1 serving*

## Screaming Banana Banchi

1   oz. banana liqueur
¾   oz. white crème de cacao
1   oz. vodka
2   ozs. half-and-half cream
1   maraschino cherry

Pour all ingredients, except cherry, over ½ cup crushed ice in blender. Blend thoroughly. Pour into 12-oz. brandy snifter. Garnish with cherry.

*Yield: 1 serving*

New Orleans, Louisiana

## Cyclone

    ozs. vodka
    ozs. passion-fruit syrup
    oz. fresh lemon juice
    orange slice
    maraschino cherry

Pour all ingredients, except orange slice and
cherry, into cocktail shaker. Shake well. Pour
over crushed ice filling 20-oz. cyclone glass.
Garnish with orange slice and cherry. Serve
with straw.

*Yield: 1 serving*

## Hurricane Punch

4   ozs. dark rum
2   ozs. passion-fruit syrup
2   ozs. fresh lemon juice
1   orange slice
1   maraschino cherry

Pour all ingredients, except orange slice and
cherry, into cocktail shaker. Shake well. Pour
over crushed ice filling 20-oz. hurricane glass.
Garnish with orange and cherry. Serve with
straw.

*Yield: 1 serving*

## Cappuccino Vivace

4   ozs. black coffee, hot
4   ozs. half-and-half cream
$\frac{3}{4}$  teaspoon cocoa
$\frac{3}{4}$  teaspoon sugar
$\frac{1}{4}$  oz. brandy
$\frac{1}{4}$  oz. rum
$\frac{1}{4}$  oz. gin
$\frac{1}{4}$  oz. light crème de cacao
$\frac{1}{4}$  oz. dark crème de cacao
$\frac{1}{4}$  oz. Galliano
    Whipped cream

In a saucepan, mix hot coffee, half-and-half, cocoa, and sugar. Heat but do not boil mixture. In a separate container, mix brandy, rum, gin, light and dark crème de cacao, and Galliano. Pour liquor mixture into 10-oz. stemmed glass. Add heated coffee mixture. Top with whipped cream. *Note*: To avoid possible breakage of the glass, pour the hot liquid over a metal spoon in the glass.

*Yield: 1 serving*

## Pfamous Pfister Pfreeze

1 oz. dry gin
$\frac{1}{2}$ oz. 151-proof rum
$\frac{1}{2}$ oz. Drambuie
1 oz. lime juice
Splash club soda
1 lime wedge
1 maraschino cherry

Pour all ingredients, except lime wedge and cherry, over 4 ozs. crushed ice in blender. Blend until slushy. Pour into double old-fashioned glass. Garnish with lime wedge and cherry.

*Yield: 1 serving*

## French 125

$1\frac{1}{2}$ ozs. brandy
$\frac{1}{2}$ oz. lemon juice
1 teaspoon powdered sugar
4 ozs. champagne, chilled
1 lemon peel strip

Place brandy, lemon juice, and powdered sugar into collins glass. Stir until sugar is dissolved. Add 4 ozs. cracked ice. Slowly pour champagne to fill. Twist lemon peel above drink and drop into glass.

*Yield: 1 serving*

# The Pied Piper

San Francisco, California

## Pied Piper Fizz

1½ ozs. dry gin
½ oz. applejack brandy
2 ozs. whipping cream
1½ ozs. fresh lemon juice
1 teaspoon superfine sugar

Place all ingredients with ice cubes in cocktail shaker. Shake well. Strain into 8-oz. glass.

*Yield: 1 serving*

## Original Pied Piper Sour in the Rough

1 orange, cut into quarters, peeled
1 lemon, cut into quarters, peeled
2 ozs. rye whiskey
2 ozs. water
1 teaspoon superfine sugar

Squeeze juice from orange and lemon quarters over ice cubes in cocktail shaker. Drop orange and lemon quarters into shaker. Add whiskey, water, and sugar. Shake well. Pour into large glass.

*Yield: 1 serving*

# THE **Pimlico**
# **Hotel**
## The Cavalier Lounge

Baltimore, Maryland

## Davis Daisy

$3/4$ oz. green Chartreuse
$3/4$ oz. amaretto liqueur
$1/2$ oz. gin
$1/2$ oz. lime juice
$1/2$ oz. orange juice

Pour all ingredients into blender. Blend thoroughly. Pour over ice cubes in brandy snifter.

*Yield: 1 serving*

## Preakness

1 oz. white rum
$1/2$ oz. Jamaican coffee liqueur
$1/2$ oz. canned cream of coconut
1 orange slice
1 maraschino cherry

Pour all ingredients, except orange slice and cherry, over $1/4$ cup crushed ice in blender. Blend until creamy. Pour into brandy snifter. Garnish with orange slice and cherry.

*Yield: 1 serving*

# PIM'S PUB

Lexington, Kentucky

## Orange Pizzazz

1½  ozs. vodka
 1  oz. rum
 4  ozs. orange juice
 1  oz. whipping cream
¼  oz. orgeat
 1  orange slice
 1  maraschino cherry

Pour all ingredients, except orange slice and cherry, over crushed ice in blender. Blend thoroughly. Pour into brandy snifter. Garnish with orange slice and cherry.

*Yield: 1 serving*

# The New York Playboy Club

## Crème de Connie

$3/4$   oz. white crème de cacao
$1/2$   oz. crème de noyaux
1   oz. cream of coconut
$1\frac{1}{2}$   ozs. half-and-half cream
1   pineapple spear

Pour all ingredients, except pineapple spear, with crushed ice in blender. Blend until creamy. Pour into 8-oz. mug. Garnish with pineapple spear.

*Yield: 1 serving*

## Jo's Collins

3   ozs. champagne, chilled
$1\frac{1}{4}$   ozs. peach liqueur
2   ozs. orange juice
    7-Up

Pour champagne, liqueur, and orange juice into 8-oz. mug filled with ice. Stir slightly. Top with 7-Up.

*Yield: 1 serving*

# THE POLO LOUNGE AT
The Beverly Hills Hotel

**Beverly Hills, California**

## Planter's Punch

| | |
|---|---|
| 1¼ | ozs. light rum |
| 1¼ | ozs. fresh orange juice |
| 1¼ | ozs. fresh lemon juice |
| ⅓ | oz. grenadine |
| ½ | oz. dark rum |
| 1 | pineapple chunk |
| 1 | orange slice |
| 1 | maraschino cherry |

Pour light rum, orange and lemon juices, and grenadine over crushed ice in tall 14-oz. glass. Stir well. Float dark rum on drink. Garnish with pineapple chunk, orange slice, and cherry.

*Yield: 1 serving*

## P.T.'s Blue Angel

1½ ozs. blue curaçao
1½ ozs. triple sec
3 ozs. orange juice
7-Up

Pour all ingredients, except 7-Up, over ice in blender. Blend until slushy. Pour into tall 13-oz. glass. Top with 7-Up.

*Yield: 1 serving*

## Ron Jon

1 oz. gin
½ oz. sweet vermouth
Dash bitters
1 lemon peel strip

Pour gin, vermouth, and bitters over crushed ice in old-fashioned glass. Stir well. Twist lemon peel over drink and drop into glass.

*Yield: 1 serving*

## Peaches 'n' Cream

1    oz. peach-flavored brandy
½   cup peach slices
3    ozs. vanilla ice cream

Place all ingredients, except 1 peach slice, in blender. Blend until smooth. Pour into chilled 7-oz. sherbet glass. Garnish with peach slice.

*Yield: 1 serving*


## Hot Maxwell's

½   oz. peppermint schnapps
½   oz. chocolate liqueur
6    ozs. hot chocolate
     Whipped cream
1    teaspoon sweet chocolate, shaved

Heat but do not boil schnapps, liqueur, and hot chocolate in saucepan. Pour into 8-oz. coffee mug. Top with swirl of whipped cream. Garnish with chocolate shavings.

*Yield: 1 serving*

# THE RITZ BAR

**Boston, Massachusetts**

## White Elephant

1½  ozs. vodka
½   oz. white crème de cacao
4   ozs. milk

Pour all ingredients over ice in cocktail shaker. Shake well. Strain over ice cubes in tall 12-oz. glass.

*Yield: 1 serving*

## Tiger's Tail

1½  ozs. sweet vermouth
6   ozs. orange juice, chilled
1   lime wedge
1   orange peel strip

Mix vermouth and orange juice in cocktail shaker. Pour over ice cubes in tall 12-oz. glass. Garnish with lime wedge and orange peel.

*Yield: 1 serving*

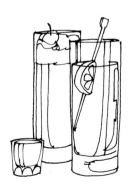

# Roark's Tavern

Monticello, New York

## Roark's Old-Fashioned

1   sugar cube
3   drops Angostura bitters
1   large lemon peel strip
3   ozs. rum
1   orange slice
1   maraschino cherry

Place sugar in old-fashioned glass. Sprinkle with bitters. Twist lemon peel above sugar and drop into glass. Fill glass with ice cubes. Add rum. Stir. Garnish with orange slice and cherry.

*Yield: 1 serving*

## Roark's Booster

1   oz. gin
½   oz. dry vermouth
    Dash orange juice
    Dash lemon juice
1   maraschino cherry

Stir gin, vermouth, and orange and lemon juices well with ice in cocktail shaker. Strain into tulip champagne glass. Garnish with cherry.

*Yield: 1 serving*

## The Flaming Hurricane

2   ozs. light rum
2   ozs. passion-fruit syrup
2   ozs. prepared sweet-and-sour mix
2   ozs. water
1   orange slice
1   sugar cube
1   teaspoon lemon extract, 80% alcohol

Pour rum, passion-fruit syrup, sweet-and-sour mix, and water into cocktail shaker. Shake well. Pour over crushed ice in tall 22-oz. glass. Place orange slice on drink. Soak sugar cube in lemon extract. Place sugar cube on orange slice. Flame and serve.

*Yield: 1 serving*

## Red Baron

3    ozs. 7-Up
2½   ozs. half-and-half cream
2    ozs. piña colada mix
1    oz. grenadine
1    maraschino cherry

Pour all ingredients, except cherry, over crushed ice in cocktail shaker. Shake well. Pour into double old-fashioned glass. Garnish with cherry.

(To make a Big Smash, add 1¼ ozs. sloe gin to the Red Baron recipe.)

*Yield: 1 serving*

# THE RUSSIAN LADY CAFE

Hartford, Connecticut

## Downtowner

1   oz. cognac
2   ozs. ginger ale
1   lemon wedge
1   lemon slice

Pour cognac and ginger ale over ice cubes in brandy snifter. Stir. Squeeze lemon wedge above drink and discard. Garnish with lemon slice.

*Yield: 1 serving*

## The Russian Sling

3     cucumber slices
1½    ozs. Pimm's Cup No. 1
2     ozs. 7-Up
1     lemon wedge

Place 1 cucumber slice in bottom of tall 14-oz. glass. Add layer of ice cubes. Place cucumber slice over ice. Add layer of ice cubes. Add Pimm's Cup No. 1. Top with 7-Up. Squeeze lemon wedge over drink and discard. Garnish with remaining cucumber slice.

*Yield: 1 serving*

## Banana Mana

1   oz. tequila
1   oz. triple sec
2   ozs. prepared sweet-and-sour mix
¼   oz. crème de bananes
2   thin banana slices, peeled

Pour tequila, triple sec, and sweet-and-sour mix over ice in cocktail shaker. Shake well. Strain into whiskey-sour glass. Float crème de bananes on drink. Garnish with banana slices.

*Yield: 1 serving*

## Kelly's Ghost

1½   ozs. vodka
½   oz. crème de menthe
1   lemon peel strip

Pour vodka and crème de menthe over crushed ice in old-fashioned glass. Stir well. Twist lemon peel above drink and drop into glass.

*Yield: 1 serving*

# The Sazerac Bar

## Bayou Swizzle

1¼ ozs. simple syrup mix*
1 drop green food coloring
1¼ ozs. golden rum
1 oz. lime juice
4 dashes Jamaican rum
1 lime slice
1 maraschino cherry

Blend simple syrup mix with food coloring in cocktail shaker. Add golden rum and lime juice. Stir well. Pour over crushed ice in tall 16-oz. glass. Float Jamaican rum on drink. Garnish with lime slice and cherry.

* **Simple Syrup Mix:** Place 3 teaspoons granulated sugar and 1 oz. water in saucepan. Cook until sugar dissolves, stirring occasionally.

*Yield: 1 serving*

## Pete's Peach

1 oz. Southern Comfort
¼ slice canned peach
1 oz. grenadine
½ oz. lime juice

Place all ingredients with 2 ozs. crushed ice in blender. Blend until smooth. Pour into champagne glass.

*Yield: 1 serving*

# $\mathcal{S}$candia
## RESTAURANT

Los Angeles, California

## Danish Bloody Mary

| | |
|---|---|
| 2 | ozs. aquavit |
| 8 | ozs. tomato juice, chilled |
| | Juice of 1 lime |
| $\frac{1}{2}$ | teaspoon Ac'cent |
| $\frac{1}{2}$ | teaspoon celery salt |
| | Dash Tabasco |
| 1 | celery rib |

Place all ingredients, except celery rib, in double old-fashioned glass. Stir well. Add ice if desired. Garnish with celery rib.

*Yield: 1 serving*


## Viking Bloody Bull

| | |
|---|---|
| 2 | ozs. aquavit |
| 4 | ozs. tomato juice, chilled |
| 4 | ozs. beef broth, chilled |
| | Juice of 1 lime |
| $\frac{1}{2}$ | teaspoon Ac'cent |
| $\frac{1}{2}$ | teaspoon celery salt |

Place all ingredients in double old-fashioned glass. Stir well. Add ice if desired.

*Yield: 1 serving*

# Shenanigan's

Phoenix, Arizona

## Pineapple Francine

        2   ozs. rum
    1½  ozs. apricot-flavored brandy
        1   oz. pineapple juice
        1   oz. whipping cream
        1   oz. canned crushed pineapple

Place all ingredients with crushed ice in blender. Blend until smooth. Pour into 12-oz. brandy snifter.

*Yield: 1 serving*

## Shenana-Banana

        1   oz. Swiss chocolate almond liqueur
      ¾   oz. crème de bananes
    1½  ozs. whipping cream
      ½   banana, peeled and sliced
            Whipped cream
        1   maraschino cherry

Place all ingredients, except whipped cream and cherry, with ice in blender. Blend until smooth. Pour into 12-oz. brandy snifter. Top with swirl of whipped cream. Garnish with cherry.

*Yield: 1 serving*

## Pick Me Up José

1    oz. white or gold tequila
1    orange slice
$\frac{1}{4}$   teaspoon sugar
$\frac{3}{4}$   oz. 151-proof rum

Place tulip champagne glass on saucer. Pour tequila into glass. Place orange slice on rim of glass and sprinkle with sugar. Pour rum over orange slice, allowing some rum to run down into saucer. Ignite rum in saucer. Blow out flame when it reaches top of glass. Alternate sips of tequila with bites of orange slice.

*Yield: 1 serving*

## White Heart

1    oz. sambuca liqueur
$\frac{3}{4}$   oz. white crème de cacao
3    ozs. half-and-half cream

Pour ingredients over ice in cocktail shaker. Shake well. Strain into cocktail glass.

*Yield: 1 serving*

## Dutch Velvet

1½   ozs. chocolate mint liqueur
 1    oz. banana liqueur
 3    to 4 ozs. half-and-half cream (to taste)
 1    teaspoon sweet chocolate, shaved

Pour liqueurs and cream into cocktail shaker. Shake well. Pour into 10-oz. wineglass. Garnish with chocolate shavings.

*Yield: 1 serving*

## Hawaiian Sunset

1½   ozs. cranberry liqueur
 1    oz. orange curaçao
 1    oz. rum
 2    to 3 ozs. prepared lemon mix (to taste)
 1    orange slice
 1    pineapple chunk

Pour all ingredients, except orange slice and pineapple chunk, over ice in cocktail shaker. Shake well. Pour into 12-oz. wineglass. Garnish with orange slice and pineapple chunk.

*Yield: 1 serving*

103

# SILKEY AND MARGARET'S

Memphis, Tennessee

## Bowl Weevil

|       |                                |
|-------|--------------------------------|
| 3     | ozs. rum                       |
| 1½    | ozs. vodka                     |
| 1½    | ozs. tequila                   |
| ½     | oz. Galliano                   |
| 8     | ozs. orange juice              |
| 3     | ozs. prepared sweet-and-sour mix |
| 3     | ozs. grenadine                 |
| 2     | orange slices                  |
| 2     | maraschino cherries            |

Pour all ingredients, except orange slices and cherries, over ice cubes in cocktail shaker. Shake well. Strain over crushed ice filling 36-oz. brandy snifter. Garnish with orange slices and cherries. Serve with 2 straws.

*Yield: 2 servings*

## Silkey's Mai Tai

|       |                       |
|-------|-----------------------|
| 1½    | ozs. rum              |
| 1½    | ozs. orange juice     |
| 1½    | ozs. pineapple juice  |
| 1½    | ozs. lime juice       |
| 1½    | ozs. cherry juice     |
| 1     | lime slice            |
| 1     | maraschino cherry     |

Pour all ingredients, except lime slice and cherry, over ice cubes in tall 12-oz. glass. Stir well. Garnish with lime slice and cherry.

*Yield: 1 serving*

# TAVERN ON THE GREEN

New York, New York

## Mimosa

5  ozs. champagne, chilled
3  ozs. fresh orange juice, chilled
1  thin orange slice

Pour champagne and orange juice into chilled champagne glass. Stir slightly. Put orange slice on rim of glass.

*Yield: 1 serving*

## Sweet Prince

1   oz. 151-proof rum
3/4 oz. Cherry Heering
6   ozs. vanilla ice cream
    Splash lemon juice
    Splash half-and-half cream
    Whipped cream
1   maraschino cherry

Place all ingredients, except whipped cream and cherry, with crushed ice in blender. Blend until smooth. Pour into 18-oz. wineglass. Top with swirl of whipped cream. Garnish with cherry.

*Yield: 1 serving*


## UFO

1   oz. Mexican coffee liqueur
1   oz. amaretto liqueur
6   ozs. vanilla ice cream
    Splash half-and-half cream
    Ground cinnamon

Place all ingredients, except cinnamon, with ½ cup crushed ice in blender. Blend until smooth. Pour into 18-oz. wineglass. Garnish with cinnamon.

*Yield: 1 serving*

THOMAS LORD'S

San Francisco, California

## Panini

2   ozs. rum
6   ozs. panini mix*
1   mint sprig

Pour ingredients, except mint sprig, over ice in blender. Blend until semifrozen. Pour into 15-oz. glass. Garnish with mint sprig.

* **Panini Mix:** Place 1½ pounds bananas, peeled and sliced; 4 ozs. frozen concentrated orange juice; 2 ozs. banana liqueur; and 1½ ozs. simple syrup mix† in blender. Blend until smooth. (Makes 5 servings.)

† **Simple Syrup Mix:** Place 6 teaspoons granulated sugar and ¾ oz. water in saucepan. Cook until sugar dissolves, stirring occasionally.

*Yield: 1 serving*

## Chi Chi

2   ozs. vodka
½   oz. orange curaçao
1½  ozs. prepared sweet-and-sour mix
1½  ozs. pineapple juice
½   oz. coconut syrup
½   oz. half-and-half cream
1   pineapple chunk
1   maraschino cherry

Pour all ingredients, except pineapple chunk and cherry, over ice in blender. Blend until semifrozen. Pour into 15-oz. glass. Garnish with pineapple chunk and cherry.

*Yield: 1 serving*

# Tiffanys

Marina Del Rey, California

## Brown Bomber

3/4 oz. peanut liqueur
1/4 oz. white crème de cacao
4 ozs. half-and-half cream

Pour all ingredients over crushed ice in blender. Blend until smooth. Pour into cocktail glass.

*Yield: 1 serving*

## Tia Napoli

1 1/3 ozs. tequila
1/2 oz. Galliano
5 ozs. half-and-half cream

Pour all ingredients over crushed ice in blender. Blend until smooth. Pour into cocktail glass.

*Yield: 1 serving*

# todd's

## Sangría

3 ozs. red Burgundy
½ oz. dry sherry
½ oz. grenadine
½ oz. prepared sweet-and-sour mix
½ oz. orange juice
1 lemon peel strip
1 lime wedge
1 orange slice
1 maraschino cherry

Pour all ingredients, except lemon peel, lime wedge, orange slice, and cherry, over ice in cocktail shaker. Shake well. Strain over ice cubes in 14-oz. wineglass. Twist lemon peel above drink and drop into glass. Garnish with lime wedge, orange slice, and cherry.

*Yield: 1 serving*

## Spritzer

5 ozs. dry Chablis, chilled
  Club soda, chilled
1 lime wedge

Pour wine over ice cubes in chilled 14-oz. wineglass. Fill glass with club soda. Squeeze lime wedge over drink and drop into glass.

*Yield: 1 serving*

## Peruvian Cherry Blossom

1½  ozs. pisco brandy
½  oz. Cherry Heering
2  ozs. lemon juice
1½  teaspoons superfine sugar

Place all ingredients over ice in cocktail shaker. Shake well. Strain into whiskey-sour glass.

*Yield: 1 serving*

## Pisco Special

1½  ozs. pisco brandy
1½  ozs. anisette
1½  ozs. whipping cream
1  egg yolk
1  teaspoon superfine sugar

Place all ingredients over ice in cocktail shaker. Shake well. Strain into whiskey-sour glass.

*Yield: 1 serving*

# TRADER VIC'S

San Francisco, California

## Scorpion

| 2 | ozs. Puerto Rican light rum |
| 1 | oz. brandy |
| 2 | ozs. orange juice |
| $1\frac{1}{2}$ | ozs. lemon juice |
| $\frac{1}{2}$ | oz. orgeat |
| 1 | gardenia |

Pour all ingredients, except gardenia, over $\frac{1}{2}$ cup crushed ice in blender. Blend until smooth. Pour over ice cubes in 12-oz. champagne glass. Garnish with gardenia.

*Yield: 1 serving*

## Pogo Stick

| 2 | ozs. gin |
|   | Juice of $\frac{1}{2}$ lime |
| $\frac{3}{4}$ | oz. frozen concentrated pineapple-grapefruit juice |
| 1 | mint sprig |
| 1 | rock candy stick |

Pour all ingredients, except mint sprig and rock candy stick, over ¼ cup crushed ice in blender. Blend thoroughly. Pour over ice cubes in footed iced-tea glass. Garnish with mint sprig and rock candy stick.

*Yield: 1 serving*

# TS STATION

Shreveport, Louisiana

## Neige Caramel

1½  ozs. caramel liqueur
1   oz. light rum
5   ozs. soft vanilla ice cream
    Whipped cream

Place all ingredients, except whipped cream, in blender. Blend well. Pour into 8-oz. wineglass. Top with swirl of whipped cream.

*Yield: 1 serving*

## Caramel Nut

1   oz. crème de cacao
1   oz. caramel liqueur
5   ozs. soft vanilla ice cream
    Whipped cream
    Chopped nuts

Place all ingredients, except whipped cream and nuts, in blender. Blend until smooth. Pour into 10-oz. wineglass. Top with a swirl of whipped cream. Garnish with nuts.

*Yield: 1 serving*

THE "21" CLUB

## South Side

2  ozs. gin or vodka
   Juice of 1 lime
1  teaspoon superfine sugar
6  to 8 fresh mint leaves

   Place all ingredients with ice in cocktail shaker. Shake well to break up mint leaves. Pour into chilled cocktail glass.

*Yield: 1 serving*

the VINEYARDS

Southfield, Michigan

## Lambrusco Sour

2  ozs. Lambrusco wine
   Juice of ½ lemon
1  teaspoon superfine sugar
1  orange slice
1  maraschino cherry

   Place all ingredients, except orange slice and cherry, in blender. Blend slightly. Pour over ice cubes in old-fashioned glass. Garnish with orange slice and cherry.

*Yield: 1 serving*  115

## Washington Square
## Bar & Grill.

## Square Picon Punch

3 ozs. champagne, chilled
1 oz. Amer Picon
½ oz. brandy
1 lemon peel strip

Pour champagne and Amer Picon over ice cubes in 6-oz. wineglass. Stir slowly. Float brandy on drink. Twist lemon peel above drink and drop into glass.

*Yield: 1 serving*

## WSB&G Fizz

⅓ oz. vodka
⅓ oz. brandy
⅓ oz. crème de cacao
3 ozs. half-and-half cream
1 egg
Ground nutmeg

Place all ingredients, except nutmeg, over ice in blender. Blend briefly. Strain into 6-oz. wineglass. Garnish with nutmeg.

*Yield: 1 serving*

WINDOWS ON THE WORLD

## White Lady

1½   ozs. gin
1   oz. triple sec
1½   ozs. lemon juice
½   teaspoon superfine sugar
1   lime slice

Place all ingredients, except lime slice, over ice in cocktail shaker. Shake well. Strain over ice cubes in old-fashioned glass with sugared rim (dipped in extra lemon juice and then sugar). Garnish with lime slice.

*Yield: 1 serving*

## Red Apple

2   ozs. white wine
1¾   ozs. calvados
1   oz. grenadine
3   ozs. orange juice
1   teaspoon superfine sugar
1   mint sprig

Place all ingredients, except mint sprig, with ice in cocktail shaker. Shake well. Strain over crushed ice in 10-oz. wineglass. Garnish with mint sprig.

*Yield: 1 serving*

117

## Slushy Margarita

1¼   ozs. tequila
¾   oz. triple sec
3   ozs. prepared sweet-and-sour mix
1   lime wedge

Pour all ingredients, except lime wedge, over crushed ice in blender. Blend until thick. Pour into 15-oz. wineglass with salted rim (dipped in lime juice and then coarse salt). Garnish with lime wedge.

*Yield: 1 serving*

## Kioki Coffee

1   oz. brandy
½   oz. Mexican coffee liqueur
½   oz. crème de cacao
    Black coffee, hot
    Whipped cream
1   teaspoon sweet chocolate, shaved

Pour brandy, liqueur, and crème de cacao into 6-oz. glass with handle. Add hot coffee to within ½ inch of rim. Stir well. Top with swirl of whipped cream. Garnish with chocolate shavings. *Note*: To avoid possible breakage of the glass, pour the hot liquid over a metal spoon in the glass.

*Yield: 1 serving*

## Jessie's Chocolate Chip

³/₄ oz. chocolate mint liqueur
³/₄ oz. white crème de cacao
    Black coffee, hot
    Whipped cream

Pour liqueur and crème de cacao into large coffee mug. Fill with coffee. Stir well. Top with swirl of whipped cream.

*Yield: 1 serving*

## Patti's Blended Velvet Fondilini

½ oz. orange liqueur
½ oz. white crème de cacao
½ oz. crème de bananes
1 oz. half-and-half cream
½ oz. orange juice

Pour all ingredients over ice in blender. Blend until smooth. Strain into tall 10-oz. glass.

*Yield: 1 serving*

## BAR GLASSES

These are the basics you will need for most drinks. However, part of the "fun" for you and your guests is being flexible and imaginative in the kinds of glassware you use.

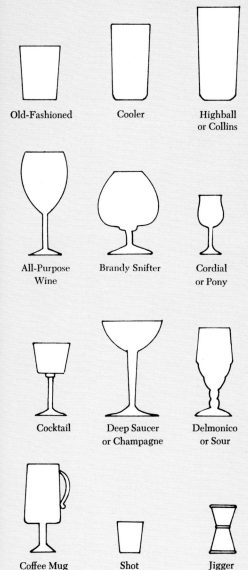

Old-Fashioned

Cooler

Highball or Collins

All-Purpose Wine

Brandy Snifter

Cordial or Pony

Cocktail

Deep Saucer or Champagne

Delmonico or Sour

Coffee Mug

Shot

Jigger

## BAR INDEX

### ALASKA

**Anchorage,** *Elevation 92,* 1007 West Third Avenue, (907-277-4336). Fogcutter, Bubble Gum, page 41.

### ARIZONA

**Phoenix,** *Shenanigan's,* 355 West Camelback, (602-266-0066). Pineapple Francine, Shenana-Banana, page 101.

**Scottsdale,** *Bobby McGee's Conglomeration,* 7043 East McDowell Street, (602-947-5757). Malibu Wave, Silver Cloud, page 15.

### CALIFORNIA

**Beverly Hills,** *Nick's Fishmarket,* 9229 Sunset Boulevard, (213-550-1544). Golden Eye, page 74.

**Beverly Hills,** *The Polo Lounge,* Beverly Hills Hotel, 9641 Sunset Boulevard, (213-276-2251). Planter's Punch, page 88.

**Beverly Hills,** *The Saloon,* 9390 Little Santa Monica Boulevard, (213-273-7155). Banana Mana, Kelly's Ghost, page 97.

**Los Angeles,** *Carlos 'n Charlie's,* 8240 Sunset Boulevard, (213-656-8830). Charlie's Freeze, Spanish Martini, page 23.

**Los Angeles,** *Casey's,* 613 South Grand Avenue, (213-629-2353). Tica, Irish Spring, page 24.

**Los Angeles,** *Scandia Restaurant,* 9040 Sunset Boulevard, (213-272-9521). Danish Bloody Mary, Viking Bloody Bull, page 99.

**Los Angeles,** *Yesterdays,* 1056 Westwood Boulevard, (213-479-4131). Slushy Margarita, Kioki Coffee, page 119.

**Marina Del Ray,** *Tiffanys,* 405 East Washington Street, (213-822-1595). Brown Bomber, Tia Napoli, page 109.

**Mission Bay,** *Cargo Bar,* San Diego Hilton Hotel, 1775 East Mission Bay Drive, (714-276-4010). Maui Christmas, page 21.

**Newport Beach,** *Blackbeard's,* 4250 Martingale Street, (714-833-0080). Pirate Grog, Yellow Strawberry, page 11.

**San Francisco,** *The Balboa Cafe,* 3199 Filmore Street, (415-921-3944). Uncle Bob's Daiquiri, California Root Beer Float, page 8.

**San Francisco,** *Blue Boar Inn,* 1713 Lombard Street, (415-567-8424). Blue Boar Nun, French Coffee, page 13.

**San Francisco,** *Buena Vista,* 2765 Hyde Street, (415-474-5044). Irish Coffee, page 19.

**San Francisco,** *Crisis Hopkins,* Three Embarcadero Center, (415-397-4866). Crisis Cocktail, Bag Dad By The Bay, page 33.

**San Francisco,** *Le Central,* 453 Bush Street, (415-391-2233). Perroquet, Chamonix, page 55.

**San Francisco,** *Perry's,* 1944 Union Street, (415-922-9022). Cappuccino Vivace, page 80.

**San Francisco,** *The Pied Piper,* Sheraton Palace Hotel, 639 Market Street, (415-392-8600). Pied Piper Fizz, Original Pied Piper Sour in the Rough, page 83.

**San Francisco,** *Thomas Lord's,* 150 Chestnut Street, (415-563-3303). Panini, Chi Chi, page 108.

**San Francisco,** *Trader Vic's,* 20 Cosmo Place, (415-776-2232). Scorpion, Pogo Stick, page 113.

**San Francisco,** *Washington Square Bar & Grill,* 1707 Powell Street, (415-982-8123). Square Picon Punch, WSB & G Fizz, page 116.

**Santa Barbara,** *Maggie McFly's Saloon,* 536 State Street, (805-966-4412). McFlying Saucer, Carmel Fog, page 60.

**Santa Barbara,** *Teaser's,* 1533 State Street, (805-966-4263). Sweet Prince, UFO, page 107.

**Sausalito,** *The Alta Mira Bar,* Alta Mira Hotel, 125 Bulkley Avenue, (415 332-1350). Alta Mira Special Ramos Fizz, Coffee Alta Mira, page 1.

**Sausalito,** *Zack's,* Bridgeway & Turney Streets, (415-332-9779). Jessie's Chocolate Chip, Patti's Blended Velvet Fondilini, page 120.

## COLORADO

**Aspen,** *The Paragon,* 419 East Hyman, (303-925-7499). Smith & Kearns, Screaming Banana Banchi, page 77.

**Boulder,** *Bananas!,* 3161 Walnut, (303-449-5300). Strawberry Banana Split, Lola Granola, page 9.

**Denver,** *Bull & Bush,* 4700 Cherry Creek Drive South, (303-399-0474). Strawberry Slush, page 20.

**Denver,** *The Colorado Mine Company,* 4490 East Virginia, (303-321-6555). The Zamboanga Hummer, The Coming and Going, page 30.

**Denver,** *The Lift,* 4501 East Virginia, (303-377-2701). The Lift Cooler, Spanish Coffee, page 57.

**Denver,** *London House,* 3875 Cherry Creek Drive South. (303-399-0474). Hogan & Burns, page 59.

**Vail,** *Bully III,* 20 Meadow Drive, (303-476-3284). Jack's Casting Couch, page 20.

**Vail,** *Donovan's Copper Bar,* Bridge Street, (303-476-5209). Snowshoe, Kamikaze, page 39.

## CONNECTICUT

**Hartford,** *The Russian Lady Cafe,* 191 Ann Street, (203-525-3003). Downtowner, The Russian Sling, page 95.
**New London,** *The Ship's Wheel,* 182 Captain's Walk, (203-442-9433). Dutch Velvet, Hawaiian Sunset, page 103.

## DISTRICT OF COLUMBIA

**Washington, D.C.,** *The Apple Tree,* 1220 19th Street, N.W., (202-223-3780). Banana Tree, Hot Peppermint Pattie, page 3.

**Washington, D.C.,** *Brickskeller Saloon,* Marifax Hotel, 1523 22nd Street, N.W., (202-293-1885). Bricklayer, Outstanding Alexander, page 17.

Washington, D.C., *Mr. Smith's,* 3104 "M" Street, N.W., (202-333-3104). Ice in Heaven, Iguana, page 72.

# FLORIDA

Coconut Grove, *The Mutiny,* The Hotel Mutiny at Sailboat Bay, 2951 South Bayshore Drive, (305-442-2400). Whoopsie Daisy, page 74.

Fort Lauderdale, *Marina Bay,* 2175 State Road 84, (305-791-7600). Cherry Bomb Fireworks, Marina Bay's Knuckle Punch, page 64.

Miami, *Cye's Rivergate,* 444 Brickell, (305-358-9100). Cye's Moustache, Cye's Coffee, page 35.

Miami Beach, *The Forge,* 432 Arthur Godfrey Road, (305-538-8533). Anvil, Forge Special, page 43.

North Miami, *The Cricket Club,* 1800 Northeast 114 Street, (305-893-6200). The Cricket, Big Apple, page 32.

Orlando, *Rosie O'Grady's,* 129 West Church Street, (305-425-7563). The Flaming Hurricane, Red Baron, page 94.

# GEORGIA

Atlanta, *Charley Magruder's,* 6300 Powers Ferry Road, (404-955-1157). Jelly Bean, Georgia Bulldog, page 25.

Atlanta, *Clarence Foster's,* 1919 Peachtree Street, N.E., (404-351-0002). Egbert, Foster's Banana, page 27.

Atlanta, *Harrison's on Peachtree,* 2110 Peachtree Road, N.W., (404-351-7596). Traffic Light, Morning After, Peachtree Cooler, page 49.

Atlanta, *Mimi's,* Omni International Hotel, 190 Marietta Street, (404-688-5900). Mimi's Peach Daiquiri, page 71.

# ILLINOIS

Chicago, *Arnie's,* 1030 North State Street, (312-266-4800). Café Freeze, Peach Treat, Ice Palace, page 7.

Chicago, *Butch McGuire's,* 20 West Division Street, (312-337-9080). Harvey Wallbanger, page 21.     125

**Chicago,** *The Lion Bar,* Continental Plaza Hotel, 909 North Michigan Avenue, (312-943-7200). Lion Tamer, Lioness, page 58.

**Chicago,** *Mrs. O'Leary's,* Hyatt Regency Chicago Hotel, 151 East Wacker Drive, (312-861-1355). Gibson Girl, Pepper's Punch, page 73.

## IOWA

**Des Moines,** *Court Avenue Station,* 625 South Court Avenue, (515-244-4410). Cowcatcher, Lil' Red Caboose, page 31.

## KANSAS

**Wichita,** *Lettuce,* 458 Waco, (316-263-1043). Lettuceade, Chocolate Snow Bear, page 56.

## KENTUCKY

**Lexington,** *Pim's Pub,* Hyatt Regency Hotel, 400 West Vine, (606-254-4444). Orange Pizzazz, page 85.

**Louisville,** *Hasenour's,* 1028 Barrett Avenue, (502-451-5210). Brave Bull, Mint Julep, Gin Buck, page 50.

## LOUISIANA

**New Orleans,** *Pat O'Brien's,* 718 Peter Street, (504-525-4823). Cyclone, Hurricane Punch, page 79.

**New Orleans,** *Sazerac Bar,* Fairmont Hotel, 123 Baronne Street, (504-529-7111). Bayou Swizzle, Pete's Peach, page 98.

**Shreveport,** *TS Station,* 750 Shreveport & Barksdale Highway, (318-865-3594). Neige Caramel, Caramel Nut, page 114.

## MARYLAND

**Baltimore,** *The Cavalier Lounge,* The Pimlico Hotel, 5301 North Park Heights Avenue, (301-664-8014). Davis Daisy, Preakness, page 84.

**Columbia,** *Clyde's,* 10221 Wincopin Circle, (301-730-2828). Hollywood Hot, May Punch, page 29.

## MASSACHUSETTS

**Boston,** *Daisy Buchanan,* 240 Newbury Street, (617-247-8516). Irish Brogue, Daisy Pardi, page 36.

**Boston,** *The Ritz Bar,* Ritz- Carlton Hotel,
15 Arlington Street, (617-536-5700).
White Elephant, Tiger's Tail, page 92.

**Newton Upper Falls,** *The Mill Falls,* 383
Elliot Street, (617-244-3080). Ginger
Snap Cocktail, The Mill Falls Special,
page 71.

**Provincetown,** *The Mews,* 359 Commercial
Street, (617-487-1500). Pear Cream,
Georgianna, Vermouth Cassis, page 70.

## MICHIGAN

**Birmingham,** *Archibald's,* 555 South
Woodward, (313-642-9400). Hummer,
Manfred's Sour Nail, page 5.

**Southfield,** *the Vineyards,* 29230 Franklin
Road, (313-355-4474). Lambrusco Sour,
page 115.

## MISSOURI

**Kansas City,** *Annie's Santa Fe,* 100 Ward
Parkway, (816-753-1621). Annie's Piña
Colada, Frozen Strawberry Margarita
page 2.

## NEVADA

**Las Vegas,** *The Brewery,* 3824 Paradise
Road, (702-731-1050). Blue Barrel,
Brewer's Nun, Brewer's Racker, page 16.

## NEW YORK

**Monticello,** *Roark's Tavern,* 14 Landhill
Avenue, (914-794-9742). Roark's Old-
Fashioned, Roark's Booster, page 93.

**New York,** *Charley O's,* 33 West 48th
Street, (212-582-7141). Irish Gremlin,
Emerald Isle Cooler, page 26.

**New York,** *Dobson's,* 341 Columbus
Avenue, (212-362-0100). Dobson's
Monkey, Toasted Almond Bar, Colorado
Road, page 37.

**New York,** *The Four Seasons,* 99 East 52nd
Street, (212-754-9495). The Four Seasons'
Strawberry Summer Cooler, Viennese
Hussar, page 45.

**New York,** *Landmark Tavern,* Chelsea
Restaurant, 108 West 18th Street,
(212-243-5644). Irish Tea, Hot Buttered
Rum, page 53.

**New York,** *Maude's,* Summit Hotel, 51st Street & Lexington Avenue, (212-752-7000). Avalanche, Maude's Berry Bomb, page 67.

**New York,** *Maxwell's Plum,* 320 East 65th Street, (212-628-2102). Fresh Framboise Champagne, Fresh Mint Daiquiri, page 69.

**New York,** *Oak Bar,* Plaza Hotel, 59th Street & Fifth Avenue, (212-759-3000). Atlantic Breeze, Troika Cocktail, page 75.

**New York,** *The Playboy Club,* 5 East 59th Street, (212-752-3100). Crème de Connie, Jo's Collins, page 87.

**New York,** *Tavern on the Green,* Central Park West at 67th Street, (212-873-3200). Mimosa, page 106.

**New York,** *Top of the Park,* 1 G & W Plaza, (212-333-3800). Peruvian Cherry Blossom, Pisco Special, page 112.

**New York,** *The "21" Club,* 21 West 52nd Street, (212-582-7200). South Side, page 115.

**New York,** *Windows on the World,* 1 World Trade Center, (212-938-1111). White Lady, Red Apple, page 117.

## OHIO

**Cincinnati,** *The Blind Lemon,* 936 Hatch Street, (513-241-3885). Surber's Revenge, Bower's Excursion, Howard's Surprise, page 12.

**Cincinnati,** *Maisonette,* 114 East 6th Street, (513-721-2260). Kir, Café Brûlot, page 63.

**Cleveland,** *Market Street Exchange,* 2516 Market Street, (216-579-0520). Cherry Blizzard, Coconut Toastie, page 65.

## PENNSYLVANIA

**Philadelphia,** *Downey's,* 526 South Front Street, (215-629-0526). Downey's Orange Creme, Sparkling Jack Apple, page 40.

**Philadelphia,** *Fran O'Brien's,* 4190 City Line Avenue, (215-473-0300). Volga Boatman, Fran's-Sicle, page 46.

**Philadelphia,** *Jimmy's Milan,* 39 South 19th
Street, (215-563-2499). Jill's Stinger,
Sunbeam, page 52.

**Philadelphia,** *P.T.'s,* 6 South Front Street,
(215-922-5676). P.T.'s Blue Angel, Ron
Jon, page 89.

**Philadelphia,** *Shippens,* 701 Fourth Street,
(215-925-2325). Pick Me Up José,
White Heart, page 102.

## TENNESSEE

**Memphis,** *T.G.I. Friday's,* 2115 Madison,
(901-274-0671). Gorilla Punch, Bob
Cratchit's Cup, page 47.

**Memphis,** *Silkey and Margaret's,* 2106
Madison, (901-726-4565). Bowl Weevil,
Silkey's Mai Tai, page 105.

## TEXAS

**Dallas,** *The Filling Station,* 6001 Skillman,
(214-691-4488). Grease Job, Anti-Freeze,
page 42.

**Dallas,** *Houlihan's Old Place,* 4 North Park
East, (214-361-9426). Tequila Sunrise,
Houlihan's Sangría, page 51.

**Dallas,** *R. G. Maxwell's,* 13020 Preston
Road, (214-387-2911). Peaches 'n'
Cream, Hot Maxwell's, page 91.

**Houston,** *Todd's,* 5050 Richmond Avenue,
(713-626-5990). Sangría, Spritzer,
page 111.

**San Antonio,** *Magic Time Machine,*
902 N.E. Loop 410, (512-828-1478).
Italian Delight, Velvet Hammer, page 61.

## WASHINGTON, D.C.: see District of
Columbia.

## WISCONSIN

**Milwaukee,** *Crown Room,* The Pfister
Hotel & Tower, 424 Wisconsin,
(414-273-8222). Pfamous Pfister Pfreeze,
French 125, page 81.

## DRINK RECIPE INDEX

Some drinks are made with equal amounts of several liquors. For your convenience these drinks are listed under more than one liquor category.

## BRANDIES

## GIN

## LIQUEURS

## RUMS

## TEQUILAS

## VODKA

## WHISKIES

## WINES

## HOT DRINKS

## NONALCOHOLIC